Holding On, Letting Go...

Holding On, Letting Go...

Kirtipriya Jha

PAPER TOWNS
PUBLISHERS

PAPER TOWNS
PUBLISHERS

First published by
Papertowns Publishers
72, Vishwanath Dham Colony,
Niwaru Road, Jhotwara,
Jaipur, 302012

Holding On, Letting Go

ISBN Print Book – 978-81-19455-47-8

Printed in India

Cover Design by The Book Story
@aditicshah01@gmail.com

Hey You,

We meet hundreds of strangers every day, but only a handful have any impact on us and very rarely someone has the capability to turn our world around. I am not sure how to say this to you, but you are one such person and now even if when we aren't together, you will be one of the best part of my journey so far, you will always remain my favourite hello and one of my hardest goodbye and you might be long gone, and I am not sure if these words will ever reach you, but a part of me will always love you, a part of me will always belong to you, and even if I try to forget it all, I never will because your name is tattooed on my soul. And you might regret it all now, maybe feel sorry about it too, but you know I can never feel the same way, cause if I was given a chance, I would do everything exactly the same, all over again.

I wonder if you ever wonder had we not fallen apart how far have we had gone. Would we have loved each other differently knowing we had so little time or had everything been still the same. I know I would have loved you differently, cause somehow, I feel like I never loved you with everything that I had and that makes me regret the things I should have done when I was with you, but I guess it was an unending loop cause the reason to love you never ceases to exist.

I wonder 40 years from now, when we might have long forgotten everything and when you are content with your life, will you ever wonder about me, will you ever think of what I am doing and when we look at the same sky above do I ever think about you. Will we ever meet again, and if we do, will you recognize me or just pretend to be strangers. I wish, somewhere down the line we meet again, and I get to see you happy and really satisfied, I really wish I do. I Have been praying for you and rooting for you hoping all your dreams come true cause you deserve all the happiness in the world.

Yours Sincerely,

Yet another ex who still can't get over you...

Why

Why make any memory,
When what we have is temporary,

Why kiss me hard every night,
When eventually we will loose this fight,

Why show me the stars,
When you are too afraid to show your scars,

Why show me any care,
When you are not planning to be there,

Why would you smile at me,
When you can forget me so easily,

Why would you even like me,
When you know it would end in tragedy,

Why would you hold my hand,
When there is so much you will never understand,

Why insist on knowing my story,
When you have planned all along to leave me,

Why do you want to know my secrets,
When you have already decided to regret,

Why would you even play nice,
When one day, I will realize that all those were lies,

Why would you give me a nickname,
When for you it's just another game,

Why would you fall in love,
When I would never be enough.

You see, we shouldn't have started something which we could never end. Something which would be the doom of us. I wonder if the memories are worth it, the pain accompanying is worth it. I still wonder if you had the choice to do it all over again, would you do it all over again knowing what you had to go through, knowing how it broke you into a million pieces till you couldn't be broken anymore, tell me would you rather go back in time and choose to undo it...?

Reality

I was in the love Bubble I created,
Reminiscing all the tinkles on my skin,
Wondering what will be the next thing,
That's when the reality stuck in.

I was dreaming of all the things that can,
Or how you make my whole world spin,
Suddenly my alarm rang,
That's When the reality stuck in.

I was lost in my own thoughts,
Of what is and what could have been,
Instantly I saw you with her,
That's When the reality stuck in.

I was thinking of all the battles we fight,
And how every war together we can win,
But you can't have something which is not yours,
That's When the reality stuck in.

I was feeling so black and blue,
And my face lit up when you walked in,
But your smile was reserved for her,
That's When the reality stuck in.

I wasn't in love with you,
Cause that would be like an original sin,
But you looked at me and I forgot to breathe,
Apparently, that's when the reality stuck in...

I want a hug, and I want to hold a hand, I need a walk down the beach, and also eat at my favourite restaurant, I want to stare at the stars, but I also want to sleep. I want to talk way too much, and also want someone who is mine to keep, I want to travel the world, and I want to get drunk and walk down the streets, and want to meet a stranger who is sweet, but tell me if it is too weird if I want to do all of this with you…? Cause maybe I am still living in an illusion I created in my head, cause in my dreams, you still whisper that you love me. Call me sadist, for I believe it to be true.

Hard To Forget...

Your twinkling eyes and your smile,
Everything so hard to forget,
I might not talk to you,
But I still stalk you on the internet,

And sometimes I miss you so bad,
So I re read all the messages you sent,
And Stay awake every night,
Reminiscing all the time we spent,

Every book I read,
Reminds me of you,
And I know you cannot listen,
But I still silently whisper I love you,

And on the days I wish I could,
Talk to you one more time,
I look at all your pictures and videos,
That's the most accepted paradigm,

Good humor and perfect body,
And your voice is my favourite melody,
And on the nights when I wished to lie beside you,
I stay awake thinking about you and me,

And the stars in my sky,
Don't shine brighter than your eyes,
And you hold my hand and kiss me goodnight,
But you disappear by the sunrise,

And on the days when nothing is going well,
A hug from you is all I need,
And maybe you are the only antidote for,
Every word that I bleed,

You were never mine to begin with,
But I thought maybe someday,
You will have your hands wrapped around me,
And you won't be walking away,

So, if parallel universes do exist, I hope that at least one of my versions is lucky enough to end up with you and I can't wait to meet her and tell her how lucky she has been. I can't wait for her to tell me how perfect you are and how her dreams really came true and how the life she lived was everything you both hoped for. I can't wait for her to tell me every single detail of her life and I bet it would be the best love story I ever heard.

Never the Same

You and I will never be the same,
Two strangers under the same name,

In a desperate attempt to hold on to you,
I would ruin my life and you know it too,

Still missing the feel of your touch,
Will it be wrong to say I still love you so much,

Your eyes still send shivers down my spine,
Still aching for the days I could call you mine,

Your arms happen to be my safe place,
Will you be there if I need you just in case,

Your voice is as soothing as it can be,
Like our hands fitting in so perfectly,

That smile of yours that I still crave,
I was the trouble and you were my save,

I was lost in the dark and you were my light,
But maybe I just wasn't worth your fight,

Maybe I was lost in a dream pretending it to be reality,
Never knew that our story would end up in such tragedy,

Now that you are not here with me,
I hope that you now don't have to worry,

Cause I was never the one for you,
And somehow you knew it too.

You see, nothing except you ever made sense, Like I had these custom-made choices so that I could find you, so that you could turn my world around. Cause there are things beyond my explanation, beyond my understanding, like my guardian angels are guiding me to you, and everything before you seems to be a blur, and now that you ain't here, nothing seems to be making sense, like I have lost everything I ever had, and now I have no idea how to go forward, like I forgot to live, I forgot how to breathe.

Seashell

Now that I have lost you,
I have no idea what to do,
Should I just forget you,
Or find my way crawling back to you,

Would apologizing to you make everything alright,
Or should I just hug you once and call it the night,
Maybe am not still used to such cold eyes,
Cause when they saw me they shined so damn bright,

Is it too late to say that I miss your touch,
Or your eyes that seemed to say so much,
I would love to be wrapped in your arms,
Cause no amount of it would be considered too much,

But you just wanted to be my best friend,
After all those articles that you penned,
Was it so easy for you to forget everything,
Cause one moment we were at peak and other was a dead end,

Did you feel sorry for being with me,
Or did you consider yourself guilty,
Tell me how do you do like that,
Making someone a priority and then a nobody,

Maybe I was high on the way you smell,
Or on the way you collected those seashells,
Maybe I just wanted to be lost in you,
In addition to losing my mind as well.

The memories of our story, Is like being trapped in a purgatory,
I wont be needing anyone new, I am still into you,
Everything can be wrong, but you be the lyrics to my every song,
The smell of your cigarette, there are some things you can never forget,
Still haunted by the words you said, still haunted by the promises we made,
I wish I could love you through all your despair and all your sorrow,
I Wish I could love you like there was no tomorrow....

You made me hate Love

Stuck on a love that could never be mine,
I pretend to be happy but am not even fine,

And you might not have any clue,
But am still madly in love with you,

And I use your sweater as a dream catcher,
As you know, with you it all seems better,

I'll admit that I feel so alone,
When am staring at your pictures in my phone,

Wondering how could you give up on me so easily.
But weren’t we fated to fade away slowly,

Let's just be young and stupid again,
For once you loved me simple and plain,

Maybe it was easy for you to pretend,
That we were nothing more than friends,

But when you are drunk you dial my number,
And can't remember what you said when you are sober,

It broke my heart into a million pieces,
A sequence of unending pain that never ceases,

And there isn't a place I can call home,
Even in a room filled with people I feel so alone,

I can sell my soul to devil a hundred times,
To get one chance to call you mine,

You made me believe I was unlovable,
You made me think I was oh so terrible,

You made me hate myself,
You made me hate love itself,

No, it isn't a poison pill. No, it isn't something you remember when you are happy. It is something which is hidden in that place of your brain where you keep all your precious things that are way too hard to let go and way too impossible to hold on. It is something which keeps you company on your loneliest nights and darkest days. It is something which stays with you when you are at your lowest, Something which can bring a smile on your face any day. Tell me do you have any such memory which was almost happy but then it wasn't and now you just smile at the possibility of what could have almost been…

Can I call you mine..?

Maybe we can meet again for the first time,
And everything we know can be redesigned,
We won't be ending up together anyway,
But still, can I call u mine...?

Trusting each other is all we need,
And together we can cross all the red line,
Nothing I expect will work between us,
But still can I call u mine....?

Maybe I would steal a kiss,
And everything will work out fine,
I know its impossible,
But still, Can I call u mine?

The way you try to talk through your eyes,
As if trying to give me some sort of sign,
Maybe I am not that bright either,
But still, can I call you mine...?

That smile of yours,
Tastes like all the drugs together combined,
I can never be the reason no matter how hard I try,
But still, can I call u mine...?

Of all the people that I care about most,
Your name is highlighted and underlined,
Maybe you don't like it when I say,
But still, can I call you mine...?

Maybe I will look in your eyes again,
And all the feelings I had will be redefined,
We can part our ways after that,
But still, can I call you mine...?

I am supposed to forget you,
In my life you will never again shine,
There are many things I wanna say but can't,
But still, Can I call you mine...?

Since you know the answer to everything, could you explain to me why I am feeling so lost, as if no reason is enough to exist, like everything is somehow wrong, like every word spoken has lost all its meaning, maybe I will never see the light, maybe nothing will ever be good again, your memories still driving me insane, every effort to stay away going down in drain, the memory of us still holding me up in chain, nothing will ever be able to numb this pain, but who is to be blamed..?

Emptiness

I held you tight,
For one more night,

But you forgot even my name,
Cause our feelings weren't same,

And so I promised myself I would,
Be happier than I should,

But you know what happened,
I just stood there frozen,

When you were walking away,
But I still had nothing to say,

No explanation to give,
Nothing I say would make you believe,

That you are the only peace to my chaos,
Emptiness is where your name still echoes,

You told me you wanted to do this,
But I was still hung on our last kiss,

And Everything you told me was a lie,
Cause you couldn't even look me in the eyes,

My heart was fragile and you broke it so hard,

Crushed it to core and left it permanently scarred,

How can you be my cut that always bleeds,
And still be the only one I need,

Forever isn't a word made for us,
You would agree that there is nothing left to discuss,

Maybe we should delete every memory, everything around
Then it would be like error 404 where no feelings are found,

I might never get over this,
Cause you will always remain my unfulfilled wish.

Sometimes I talk to stars and moon, about you, cause you are my favourite secret, I wonder if there is anything that I should have done differently, I wonder if you wonder the same things, I wonder what you think about me now, and I reach in some kind of trance where I am relieving those old memories again and I wonder if we ever are thinking about each other at the same time and if you do, I hope you do not regret what we had, I hope our memories bring a smile on your face, I hope you cherish it the way I do, I hope that looking back at it now, you don't regret us.

Dreams

Walked in an empty house,
Memories flooding in,
Of how bright it once was,
and smelled like coffee bean,

And the moments we had on the couch,
Of when I held you in my arms,
But it all feels so empty now,
Like the destruction after storm,

Remember how we almost kissed in the
Kitchen,
Or how we lied awake whole night on terrace,
And how you would blush crimson red,
Every time I would hold you in my embrace,

Now am lying awake, alone in my bed,
And I can still hear the sound of your feet,
Maybe I am finally going insane,
Cause I hear your voice in my head on repeat,

I wish I could run to you right now,
And hold you in my arms again,
And relive all those memories,
That keeps on playing in loop in my brain,

I wish the dreams that we had,
Could be turned in reality,
And we would end up together,

For all of our eternity.

What do I call this thing that I am feeling, like I might never find peace again, like I am lost and there is no way back, like I just lost everything that I had and all my life, I have to spend longing for you, And all my life I will be looking for traces of you in everyone I meet and yet I will never be able to love someone else because I will always be in love with you. I will never be whole again, cause a part of me will always belong to you, I don't want to be close to anyone else cause no matter how wonderful and amazing they are, they will never be you...

Kissing Strangers

Kissing strangers every night,
Trying to find you in them,
I tell them they are all unique,
But I even forget their name,

And their eyes don't mesmerize at all,
And their touch doesn't feel electrifying,
And none of them could send,
Currents down my spine,

They would say the words,
That gave me Deja vu,
But the only one who could,
Make me believe in them, was you,

Some even held my hand,
While some had stories to tell,
Nothing appealed to me anyway,
Cause I was still bounded by your spell,

Some offered cigarette,
Another offered me weed,
And even when I was high,
You were the only one I need,

They touched my body,
And I kept thinking about when you,
left me with bruises all over,
Of colors green and blue,

I wasn't in my senses,
When I called your name,
Yeah! people call me crazy,
But who is to blame,

Everyone left one by one,
Only your memories left behind,
And None of it made any sense,
When our fates weren't intertwined,

I can't describe this in words, the longing, the craving, the yearning, the strong feeling of something is missing, something is going wrong, something is not as it should be. Maybe I am just being delusional, maybe I am slowly going insane, maybe I am just dramatic, who knows, and sadly there is no way to find out..

Love is worst

And of everything I ever came across, love was the worst,
Though it was supposed to be blessing, it felt like curse,

You came in my life and swept me off my feet,
Now I look for traces of you in everyone I meet,

Maybe I just wanted someone to stay by my side,
And darling I know you tried but you were never qualified,

Every promise was meant to be broken
And the door to love yourself isn't yet open,

It wrecked me apart when it was supposed to be a bliss,
I didn't know we were meant to fall apart like this,

And trust me I tried my best not to fall for you,
Because I know it would be leaving me blue,

but my hands were tied and my heart was cold,
All I wanted was for someone to hold me close,

Snapping out of an illusion I can now see,
The one you love wasn't really me,

The road to loving you was painted in black,
And now I am so tired of all the flashbacks,

Reminiscing everything that we had,
Our memories are still driving me mad,

Moving on doesn't seem like a valid option,
Three years ain't too long to be stuck in this situation,

I know the only one at fault here is me,
But what do I do if I still love you desperately,

And maybe I was never worth anything,
For you to even consider me something,

I don't think one lifetime would be enough,
For me to forget about your love.

I was your star and you were my moon, I was your curse and you were my boon,
You were the only sun in my sky, tell me why you had to say goodbye,

Poison Pill

Keeping myself so busy,
So that I don't have to think about it,
But I hope one day,
I will know just how to walk past it,

Do you ever think about me,
Do you ever visit our place occasionally,
Maybe reminiscence about the memories,
We left so gracelessly,

The walk, the weather, the trees, the breeze,
Could these things still put you to ease,
Because I am still so lost and confused,
Trying to find what its like to be at peace,

These always raising heart rate,
I try to but I cant control it,
Maybe you know the answer to,
Why its so tragic and why I am losing it,

I can feel your hands on me still,
An effect of most dangerous poison pill,
That has got my head spinning around,
Maybe I was just looking for a void to fill,

Remember when you said you could kiss me all day,
Remember when you couldn't keep the promise next day,

Remember when you were in such a hurry,
To leave it all behind and walk away,

Everything you felt yesterday meant nothing,
Every word said is the beginning of another ending,
I should be damned for believing all the words said,
Should have known it was all just condescending,

Terrified right from the start,
That one day it will all fall apart,
Call me crazy, call me insecure,
But you weren't the one i should have trusted with my heart,

A never-ending wish list,
A wishlist we had to leave incomplete,
Maybe it was all for the good,
Cause love cant exist on this one way street,

I might pretend to be busy, I might not care about how you are and what you are doing, I might pretend to be not interested, but you know with every waking moment you are present at the back of mind and no matter how hard I try to get over you, I know that I never will cause I don't know how to stop, I don't know how to stop thinking about you, I don't know how to move on, I don't know how to let you go, I don't know if I ever will.

Broken

It scares me to know,
That you don't need me anymore,

And you moved on without me,
And nothing could make me any more happy,

But it scares me to death,
Of what will happen next,

Maybe you will find someone new,
Maybe forget about me too,

And our story will be over,
One that was supposed to last forever,

So many words left unspoken,
Two hearts beating, but still broken,

And Nothing will ever be the same,
And I'd be the one to blame,

I still write about you,
I just hope you knew,

Maybe it will get easier someday,
Or maybe it was supposed to end this way,

Maybe one day it won't hurt as much,
Maybe one day I won't crave for your touch,

someday my memory will fade away,
And everything will be in shades of grey,

And a major part of me belongs to you,
Everything ever since is in shades of blue,

And even when everything is lost and done,
I will still believe that you were the one.

Saying that I miss you would be an understatement to describe what I am feeling. I miss you so much that I feel sick physically, like there is a never-ending ache in my chest. A void that can never be filled, the pain that can never be numbed. Like an important part is missing, like a bullet hole that can never be healed, like I will never be whole again, like nothing will ever make sense again, like I will never feel alright again…

Last Seen

Every night stalking your last seen,
I wonder how long has it been,
Am I still struggling with the reality,
Or is it all a dream,

Its been ages since I heard your voice,
Being your friend was my only choice,
Guess am still scared to talk to you,
Not knowing will it be you or just some noise,

Though you say nothing has changed,
Then why do I feel so estranged,
I am trying so hard to forget it all,
But those memories just can't be erased,

I still remember that smile of your,
Like it was my personal drugstore,
Nothing seems to be working now,
When every nigh I end up crying on my bedroom floor,

Everything I do, leads me back to us,
I am still painting our picture on an empty canvas,
And I keep on running back to you again and again,
When there is nothing left to discuss.

And every time when you were walking away, and all I wanted to say was, please stay a little longer, please don't leave me just yet, cause if you leave me now, I would crumble and never be whole again. Days when we talk and all I ever want to say, is that I am still in love with you, I have been missing you for the longest time, and now that you are not here, nothing seems to be making sense, but I know its crazy, and I don't wanna loose what is left of us and so I get lost staring at you, and smiling to myself that atleast I got to see you once more, my goodbyes being replaced by take care as you should know by now, I can never really say goodbye to you.

Intoxicated

When you said I was completely crazy,
Love, baby, isn't meant to be easy,

And I completely wasted my time,
Trying to chase what wasn't mine,

Expecting everything right but the person was wrong,
He was determined to lose everything we had all along

He couldn't see past the illusion I created,
He couldn't see that he was the one I needed,

And though I was intoxicated,
Everything about him was so overrated,

honey I hold grudges for so long,
It's not you with whom I belong,

But, I didn't think it would end this way,
I never thought he would be walking away,

There was nothing we could really do,
He wasn't supposed to leave me blue,

And nothing would ever be fine,
When I am not the one calling you mine

You have no idea how soothing your smile is to me, irrespective of the days when I am able to be a front row audience or not, the hope that something somewhere would be making you smile is enough for me to get through my day. I hope you keep the things and the people that make you smile a little close and I pray that you keep smiling everyday even if I am no longer the reason for that smile anymore…

Comet

You know I went on my knees,
Proposed her with the same ring,
And when she said yes,
All I kept thinking about, is our fling.
When we promised forever,
It didn't had to turn in never ever,
And it broke my heart,
Cause I wished it was you,
Right from the very start,
Don't you feel the same,
Cause I can't see it going down the flame,
You should've said yes,
And we would have the same address,
And forever would finally exist,
And that would be on top of our list,
Is it too late to make amends,
Can't we change how it ends,
Cause I am still in love with you,
And it was, is and will always be you...

One word and I was all yours, never needed a handcuff,
Doesn't matter how much I loved you, it was never enough,
Looked for you everywhere, craving to hear your sound,
Tell me how do you find something, that doesn't want to be found,
The pieces that you break me in, is much better than the worse I have been,
I looked for peace everywhere I could, but your arms were my only serene

Fading Away

The stars in my sky are fading away,
Just like how you walked away,

And your eyes were my favourite story to read,
But I never thought it would come down to this,

And the memories I have aren't enough,
I wanted all of you, But I wasn't the one you could love,

I know you didn't promise me a forever,
But didn’t you say it will all be better,

I guess we were never meant to be,
Like it's some kind of conspiracy,

But you are all I will ever need,
To make me feel complete,

My heart still aches for that one last kiss,
I had never known that kind of bliss,

Maybe hear I love you from you one last time,
For you, there is no mountain I wouldn't climb,

Loosing myself again and again, it doesn't even make any sense any more, it was easier when I could feel nothing at all, when I would wake up everyday and there was nothing to look forward to, when I would walk with nothingness inside, cause it was a lot easier than walking with pain. It was a lot easier when I had not known love, existing was a lot easier than living with this unending ache inside.

Reset

Will you at least let me be your friend,
And I promise, I will stay till the end,

Don't give up on me just yet,
Cant we just for once hit reset,

I need you more than I know,
I care about you more than I can ever show,

Maybe we will begin it all from the start,
If you promise to not break my heart,

Maybe this time I won't fall for you,
If you promise not to fall for me too,

And though we would know how we feel,
It wont really be a big deal,

Letting you go shouldn't be the only way,
Will it be a crime if I ask you to stay,

What if we leave it all behind in the past,
Will we be able to look in each others eyes at last

Is it easier for you to not think about me,
Cause you once considered me a priority,

Its easier to not talk than to see you hurt,
Every time all my efforts turning into dirt.

Maybe we should believe in fate and leave the rest,
And lets just hope that it will workout for the best.

Just not being with you is driving me insane,
Would it be better if I close my eyes and never open them again.

If we all had a reset button where would just be able to begin everything at the start, I wonder how many would choose to press it, cause no matter where I would go, you'd be my permanent home. I wonder if I made you half as happy as you did me, if holding my hand gave you the same butterflies or was it really one sided on my part, cause you made me oh so happy, you made me feel safe, you made me feel like I am someone worthy. Maybe it was never about us, but always about how you made me feel, and I wonder if I made you feel the same…

Lie to Me

Can you please lie to me,
Say that you love me,
Cause honestly there is,
No other way to be,

you were hot but I was cool,
you were modern but I was old school,
You asked me not to fall for you,
But I did exactly what I was told not to,

You had the fire but I was the ice,
You were sugar and sweet and everything nice,
You always asked me to stay the same,
Now everything has changed except my name,

You were the truth but I was made of lies,
But I was never good at saying goodbyes,
You said you will love me always and forever,
But now I am the one who doesn't even matter,

I am jealous of every drop of alcohol that touches your lips, for they get to be where I want to be, they get to be high on love just by your touch, something which I still crave for every day, they get to be with you in your loneliest time, they get to be with you when you are happy, they get to be with you whenever you want, and I wonder if I would ever be wanted in the same way…

Havoc

I can't fall out of love ,
Nothing I did was ever enough,

I want a hug so very tight,
Never thought I would break, but I just might,

I want to cry out so loud,
Am still searching for you in every crowd,

And am still hoping that you would come back,
With you gone everything seems to be pitch black,

I am not willing to admit it,
But slowly am losing it,

And I need a hug from you just in case,
For everything to fall properly in place,

Maybe your voice can calm me down,
Because it's my most favourite sound,

Will you hold me for a little while,
Maybe walk with me for a mile,

Just you with a rose, standing in front of my door,
Honey there isn't anything else that I wished for,

Maybe then it wouldn't wreck such a havoc,
if you hold my hand before everything in me broke,

Maybe I should just leave it all behind,
Accept that I will never be able to get you off my mind,

Maybe you will always have a permanent place,
In my heart, which is a mess of a maze,

Though our hearts are, but our fates aren't aligned,
And it's such a shame when I can't even call you mine...

Listening to your favourite song on repeat, Its is not my want but what I need, Maybe it's the remedy for every word that I bleed, its addiction is stronger than weed. Can never stop over analyzing what every lyric means, can't stop thinking why you introduced this song to me, can't stop thinking about you, can't stop thinking about us, tell me why am I still stuck here when you moved on so easily …

Deja Vu

Every time I try to find something new,
It feels like deja vu,
I should have known from the start,
All I was looking for was 'you'.

I try to distract my mind,
But a voice calls from behind,
Maybe someone like you,
I am always trying to find.

Don't leave me just yet,
It is not easy to forget,
Tell me how do I not remember,
The smell of your cigarette.

I thought we were perfect together,
Just like your black jacket of leather,
Living in my own dreams and fantasy,
But I guess I should have known better.

Every moment with you is memorable,
Making everything I know questionable,
I still don't know how to convince myself,
That you leaving was inevitable,

I might have loved you fiercely,
While you might have loved just to forget me,
For you darling I was always available,
But for you I was someone easily replaceable,
I have always valued you the most,
Now I spend my time talking to your ghost,
I have always been in love with you,
Even if in the end you would ruin me too…

Nightmares

I don't wanna overthink it,
But you know I miss it,

Everything that we had,
Finding home after being a nomad,

I don't wanna confess it out loud,
but you were the only one standing by me in crowd,

And I don't even want to remember,
That once you were the only one that mattered,

I wish my memory could be erased,
Isn't that better than feeling so disgraced,

I don't want to have any memory of you at all,
I wish to delete every bit of it, however big or small,

How can I erase the feel of your touch,
Tell me how do I erase that I loved you so much,

Now that everything is in shades of blue,
Tell me how to walk away from you,

Tell me how you moved on so easily,
When you said you loved me,

I want to stop dreaming about you,
All my nightmares are turning true,

Do you ever miss me at all,
Maybe call my name under influence of alcohol,

It seems like a pool of never-ending misery,
When all we had is a distant history,

Were we always meant to fall apart,
Or were we doomed right from the start,

Nothings seems to be making sense,
When you and I have to pretend to be friends,

And you talk to me like I am some stranger,
Ask me how I am doing like its some sort of game changer,

You might be good, but I still cant lie,
What hurts the most are your silent goodbyes,

And now that everything has changed,
Why do I feel so distant and estranged.

And drowning myself in alcohol seems like an easier task, Cocaine, marijuana and weed still won't be enough to cover your name continuously echoing in my brain. Maybe I need a sleep so deep that I forget even my name but what if even that is still not enough, what if I forget everything but, your name still echoes…

Damaged

How can you be alright when I am breaking,
Do you actually don't feel anything...?

Carving your name on my skin with blade,
Every inch of my skin covered with promises we made,

Cause everything happening is crushing me from inside,
And there isn't a single place on this earth where I can hide,

Will I ever be able to leave it all behind,
Will I ever be able to get you off my mind,

You behaved like whatever happened was nothing,
Making me feel like I dreamt everything,

How were you able to walk away so easily,
Because I still get mesmerized by your sight completely,

I was drunk but it's coming back to me in instalments,
That nothing we had was permanent,

My brain knew it all along but my heart couldn't accept it,
It was damaged beyond repair nothing could fix it,

you moved on way too easily,

While I am stuck on this never-ending tragedy,

On my darkest nights your memories keep me company,
And even if we loved each other, you weren't my destiny,

Nothing will ever work, nothing will ever be fine,
Now that I can never call you mine,

Tell me how do I get rid of your memories in my brain,
When everyday I just want you to fall in love with me again,

Death would seem like a lenient penalty,
In comparison to staying away from you for all eternity.

Re-reading every messages sent, thinking if I could go back to that moment again, will I ever be able to stop myself from falling for you, cause every time I look at you I fall for you again, every time I talk to you, I realize I am not over you yet, and maybe I never will, a part of me still belongs to you, a part of me will always keep on loving you, no matter the consequences, no matter the differences, a part of me will always belong to you …

Helpless

It feels so worse,
It hurts so bad,
It may look like I am moving on,
But I miss everything we had,

I see you smiling upto someone else,
And you talk to them as you used to with me,
And I feel so lost and confused,
Staring at the blank spaces between us helplessly,

It might be hard to believe,
That I still care about you,
And you may not know about it,
But I am still madly in love with you,

I wish I could talk to you,
The way I used to before,
But I guess the connection we shared,
Doesn't even exist anymore,

And I still reminiscence about,
The things that we used to do together,
I would inhale your scent as you arrived,
And suddenly the world would seem better,

It's such a shame to know,
That I wasn't a part of your forever's list,
And how is it that,
You were on top of my every wish list,

And I am still holding onto your pieces,
Even when you are long gone,
I still consider you a priority,
While for you I am just another bygone.

Someday you will forget about me, like we were never meant to be,
But tell me what should I do, when all I keep thinking about is you,
Trying to set myself free, your memories are still holding me a prisoner,
What was the point of it all, if it wasn't meant to last forever.

Priorities

Would you let me call you mine,
even when our fates aren't intertwined,

Would you at least let me be your friend,
And stick with me until the very end,

Would you promise to fight for me,
Cause I need you desperately,

Would you ever read my eyes,
Would you forgive all my lies,

Would you hold my hand once more,
And maybe then things will go to how it was before,

Would you hold on to me,
Even when I am no longer your priority,

Would you tell me everything you feel,
And I won't tell anyone that's a deal,

Would you still try to make me smile when I am sad,
And still stand by my side when I go crazy and mad,

would you still wrap me in your arms when I am cold,
Cause we know we would be walking on a threshold,

would you still kiss me when the light goes out,
Cause you are the one I can't live without,

It wouldn't be a crime if you forget everything that happened,
But you were much better than how I had you imagined.

If it makes you happy, let it destroy you, let it damage you, let it consume you, let it ruin you, let it engulf you, entangle it with your soul, let it flow through your vein, inhale it with your every breath, drown yourself in its essence and never ever let it go…

Blank Spaces

Blank spaces between the words,
lost myself in between the worlds,

Looking for you everywhere I go,
these are the secrets now you know,

I could see everything but I played blind,
Now it seems impossible to get you off my mind,

And the pages of our story are stuck together,
I hoped that was the way we stay for forever,

Let's get drunk so I can tell you everything I want to say,
You are the only person I run too when I loose my way,

And one day you text me saying you miss me,
But next day you go back to treating me like a nobody,

And I am still training myself not to run to you,
Like I always do, whenever I need you,

And it seems like an impossible task,
Because I would be all yours if you just ask,

I tried to break every bond and end it all,
But one thought of you and back to you I'd crawl,

It feels like breaking a curse,

You expect to be free but end up worse,

And tell me what would you do,
When all your darkest nightmares turn true,

I tried running away from everything I ever knew,
But how is it that I could never run away from you,

A part of me will hold on to you forever,
A part of me will keep on hoping that it gets better,

And trust me I have tried to hate you as well,
But I am still trapped by your magic spell,

And it looks like I am walking on a very thin line,
It might look that I am okay, but am not even fine,

Everything might seem alright on the outside,
But I am slowly dying inside,

And everything I feel seems like an illusion,
And letting you go doesn't seem like a valid option.

Tell me, how you are the reason why I started hating sunsets, you are the reason why I don't listen to my favourite songs, you are the reason I can't watch my favourite movie, you are the reason I can't eat my favourite dish, you are the reason I can't visit my favourite place, you are the reason I cry myself to sleep, you are the reason I can't write anymore, you are the reason my journal is empty, you are the reason I don't believe in love anymore, you are the reason I have trust issues, you are the reason why I hate people, tell me , how are you the reason that I don't do things that used to define me anymore and I still wont ever be able to hate you...

Memories

Trying to close every door,
Erase all the memories on seashore,
maybe I was just another folklore,
But when I hug your blue sweater,
Why Doesn't it feel like you anymore...

And I am lost here without a direction,
Or maybe I was just another confession,
On the wall of meaningless connection,
Trying to find myself in your eyes reflection,
Because you and I together were perfection,

And I did not stand a chance,
when the seat was already booked in advance,
And carefree I used to dance,
Searching for you at every glance,
But it all happened in my mind, like some kind of trance,

But I don't want to loose you again,
Can't live with this ever-growing pain,
My insides raging like a hurricane,
Your memories still holding me up in chain,
For, every thought of you still drives me insane,

And maybe we were born of the same star,
As we both shared the same scar,
And though I still stumble out of bar,
Feeling useless like the ashes falling from a cigar,

But I still want to be wherever you are,

You and I weren't meant to exist, we weren't meant to look into each other's eyes, weren't meant to hold each other's hand, weren't meant to touch each other, weren't meant to kiss, we weren't meant to care for each other, you weren't meant to hold me when I was down. You and I weren't supposed to fall in love, cause we both knew it will never be enough...

Square One

Why did you had to put me back in,
if you had to break me again,

I asked you to not break my heart,
And you went ahead and did exactly that,

Don't make promises you would never keep,
Left me all alone when I was crying myself to sleep,

Whispering to me all the sweet cheesy lines,
Still cant understand what were you really trying,

Telling me that you are worth the fight,
And stepping away when you had the chance to do it right,

Trying to hold my hand when the lights were on,
Cause you knew how to leave when the brightness was gone,

When everything was done and said,
You crushed my wishes with the swipe of your blade,

I gave you my heart in perfect condition,
Now that I receive it back why is it so broken,

How could you break a person so easily,
Like you never felt anything for anybody,

And I thought I had moved on,
But one text from you and am back at square one,

My heart is trying to fill a void that doesn't exist, at least not in this life, but it feels like these voids have been existing from a very long time, like they have been existing before these bodies were formed, before you and I met, before we tried to fill each other's empty spaces, they are ancient, holding the pain of a number of lifetimes, the pain of every time we had to leave each other, the pain of every time we almost were, and then we weren't.

Over You

Years have passed and it feels like yesterday,
Maybe am still stuck on the night of that Friday,

When you said let us cross the bridge,
I never anticipated it would scar me like this,

Every contact made thereafter was the result of guilt,
Well, it was way too easy to crumble what we built,

I could never stop the tears that would flow,
Every word spoken felt like a death blow,

I wonder if you ever thought of what I would do,
Cause oh boy! I might never actually get over you,

And you were the first to leave when I just stood there,
Now you come asking questions , that just ain't fair,

Why do we keep meeting at the bridge that we have already crossed,
Why do we keep trying to built something that has already been lost,

Cause everything could change but your eyes won't lie,
But now they can't bring this dead being back to life,

Though the apologies seem to be well intended,
But what's broken can never be mended,

The houses are burned, no memories left behind,
But if I told you that I am over you, I was clearly lying,

Cause you know I will ruin myself for you completely,
You know there is no one else I would want to be in love with me,

And if I don't have you, I would rather not fall in love at all,
Cause no one would ever be worth the fall.

Why do you feel like the anchor keeping me alive, like I am asphyxiating and you are my last breath, why does one msg from you bring me so much peace, one conversation is like the oxygen I needed for my soul, one meet is like you are bringing the dead me back to life, one eye contact is like the much needed soothing my soul needed, one touch is like a bliss I might never experience again...

Your Essence

I wish I could forget it all,
No matter how big or small,
Every memory of you,
Every time I wasn't worth your fall,

Everything ceased to exist,
With every cut deep in my wrist,
And you seemed so distant somehow,
Like you are all covered in mist,

But it was you who disappeared,
When I was still standing there,
And you moved on without a word,
Maybe coz it was just another illicit affair,

I was drunk on something stronger than love,
But I guess it still wasn't enough,
And I could be begging for you to stay,
But I will never be the one you think of,

And it still doesn't make any sense,
When I am drowning in your essence,
You mean the world to me but,
For you I was just another obsolescence,

and my heart was beating fast,
a feeling that wouldn't last
I wonder when will the effect wear off,
Of the magic spell which you cast.

Tell me what do I do with the part of you that's left in me, no matter how hard I try to hide it away it still shows, no matter how hard I try to leave it all behind it still comes back to haunt me. A part of you that I can't seem to hold on, a part of you that I can't seem to let go. Maybe I am addicted to all the wrong things, and maybe nothing will ever make any sense, maybe I will have to live all my life under a false pretense.

Tears

broken promises and lies been told,
Not everything that glitters is gold,

Broken heart and crying all alone,
Pictures that I can never delete from my phone,

And I am wishing on every star,
That it would mend my broken heart,

I cannot stop the tears that flow,
Every night on my pillow,

With every cut deep in my wrist,
It's addictive and I can't resist,

A few sleeping pills ain't enough,
Nothing could release me from your handcuff,

I get high and loose my senses,
But I still wait for you on all those empty benches,

Getting drunk and lost looking for you,
Trying to validate the feelings which weren't true,

All the sleepless nights waiting to hear back,
Love was long lost on this one way track,

Nothing is ever going to work,
Nothing will ever numb this hurt,

Will I ever be able to find a way out,
The silence in my head is mind numbingly loud.

But every memory of you still stays,
And in a never-ending loop it still plays,

And I might be lying in arms of someone else,
But how are you still my comfort place,

You were made of stars, but I was the cloud,
Why do I still see your face in every crowd,

Maybe I was supposed to lose it all,
Maybe I wasn't worth it after all,

Maybe just existing will one day be considered enough, because I don't think I can do anything else anymore. Couse I don't want to crave for you anymore, I don't want to yearn for your touch, I don't want to long to listen to your voice, I don't want to wish to hold your hand in mine again, I don't want to wait to look in your eyes, I don't want to dream of you again, I don't want to desire to fall for you again, I would rather not feel anything at all rather than feeling so much pain, and I don't know if I do anything else, I would rather just die, than existing like this...

Destruction

I didn't want to walk away,
I wish you would have asked me stay,
Cause I was willing to fight it all,
But you decided to push me away,

Though a periodic check seems nice on your part,
But do you ever wonder what set us so apart,
And though you might feel so sorry about it now,
But I guess it was way too easy to break my heart,

And Everything we did lead to our destruction,
When we were just looking for Salvation,
And though we thought we made each other happy,
But don't you think it was all lost in translation,

And now that we are strangers again,
Your memories still holding me up in chain,
Forgetting you doesn't seem to be working,
As you are the only thing stuck in my brain,

Maybe we had to destroy each other repeatedly,
In order to reach where we are now recently,
And though we try to get back to square one,
It seems impossible even though we loved insanely,

Though we were scared that we will loose each other,
And nothing seemed to be going better,
The feeling of loosing you never really went away,
Even when I was wrapped in your blue sweater,

But the havoc you feared was already created,
All the promises we made already truncated,
There is no point turning around now,
Cause everything, we had is already exterminated.

I wish walking away was as easy as walking in, I wish falling out was as easy as falling in, I wish forgetting you was as easy as remembering you, I wish it was easier to break a habit, I wish it was easier to get rid of being addicted to someone, I wish we could close our eyes and remember how to be happy again, I wish one day we open our eyes and we don't have to spend it longing for someone who doesn't want us, I wish we never fall for someone who isn't meant to be ours.

Like I do

Do you ever listen to my favourite song,
And miss me, like I do?

Do you ever think about me,
And wish nothing would have changed, like I do?

Do you ever read our conversation,
And wish we could talk the same, like I do?

Do you ever long to hear my voice,
And wish you could just call, like I do?

Do you ever look at our pic,
And smile stupidly at the memories, like I do?

Do you ever wish that in some parallel universe,
You and I end up together, like I do?

Do you ever crave to see me,
wishing if you could capture every moment, like I do?

Do you ever think about all of it ,
And wish if it could have been any different, like I do?

Do you ever spent sleepless nights,
Just because you cant stop crying, like I do?

Do you ever hug your pillow too tight,
imagining me instead of pillow, like I do?

Do you whisper, that you love me,
when my thought crosses your mind, like I do?

Do you ever wonder how it would feel like,
To hold my hand in yours again, like I do?

Do you ever feel like you could hug me really tight,
maybe for one last time, like I do?

Do you ever wish if nothing between us,
would had ever changed, like I do?

Do you ever wonder what it would be,
had you not walked out on me, like I do?

Do you ever wonder, if everything would be better,
Had you never met me at all, like I do?

Its like I am hanging on a thread with thorns for life, the tighter I hold, the more hurt I get, however I cannot leave it either, it's a dilemma I can never solve, it's a riddle with no correct answer, it's a puzzle with no possible solution. The memories you left with me can't be deleted, but I can't hold on to it either, it is just a painful reminder of everything that could have been, of everything we were, and everything now we are not.

Void

The damage done was permanent,
Everything happening was unfortunate,

You don't have to be sorry,
I wasn't a part of your story,

Stuck in your dream hitting rewind,
It's not easy to get you off my mind,

You promised me a date,
I guess it wasn't in my fate,

So you left me hanging in the dark,
But your remnants stuck with me like a birthmark,

Can't replace the part of me that you stole,
And now I am left here without a soul,

You left me with a void I can never fill,
And moments I treasured turned out to be suicide pill,

Why did you had to tell me that you love me,
When you planned it all along to leave me,

I am crushed into so many billion pieces now,
Can't even gather myself cause I don't know how,

But it is not your fault at all,
Maybe I wasn't worth it after all,

Can I hold on to you a little longer, even if you don't. Can I still be in love with you a little longer even if you aren't, can I still call you mine cause I might never get over the idea that you are not, Can I just keep remembering you even when you might have long forgotten what we were cause you know what is worse than being strangers, being strangers with memories that you can never forget.

Alone, again...

Running in circles with the confusion,
With no plausible solution,
thank you for the clarification,
Now I don't need any justification,

Thank you for leaving me at exhaust,
Now I know what I have lost,
I was never worth the cost,
And now I am colder than the frost,

Now I know that you never loved me enough,
Everything you said was a bluff,
I was a free bird and you were my handcuff,
My intoxication increasing with your every puff,

Now my soul is completely decayed,
for nothing of me is left to be saved,
Your name still deeply engraved,
Your treachery has me eternally enslaved.

You know what destruction is? Destruction is when a person craves to talk to you, to hear your voice, but cant, destruction is when you cannot do the things you used to because it still reminds you of them, destruction is when all the places you are visiting, you wish you were visiting it with them, destruction is when you want to share everything with them but cant, destruction is when all you do is keep thinking about them but you don't even know if you ever cross their mind even once, destruction is when all you ever wanted was to be with them, but they never wanted you…

Goodbye

I have said so many words that I am already regretting,
I understand if you don't want to speak, but it's a little upsetting,

I know apologies do not make anything right,
But doesn't everything broken deserves a fight,

But you ask me questions I can never answer,
Cause you are intelligent enough to decipher,

That I can never ever hate you,
That a part of me will always be in love with you,

But tell me if you are afraid to face the truth,
Or is it just another form of entertainment for you,

When you shoot me yet another apology out of the blue,
Is it yet another psychological analogy you are trying to do,

Cause apologies do come together with a promise,
That is provided that you are being honest,

Or maybe it's just the alcohol talking,
Cause sober you would never be calling,

Cause i keep waiting for you to talk to me one more time,

As I have been missing you now for a very long time,

You act like you have moved on and that you don't care,
You act like you are such a player,

But tell me do you ever think about me at night,
Do you ever wonder if we deserved a fight,

Do you think this was the perfect ending,
When what you do is torturously excruciating,

Cause every silence from you feels like another heartbreak,
And I am not sure how much more of it I can take,

And I was never good at saying goodbyes,
Cause every time I do, something inside surely dies.

You have been a permanent place for so long in my brain that I don't think there was a day when I didn't know you. And so I don't really know how to let go of something which has been holding such an important place in my life for as long as I can remember, I just can't say goodbye, especially to you, because when I don't, it leaves me with a hope that this is not the end, and some chapter is pending to write, but goodbye feels like an end altogether, an end I am not ready to face yet, an end I might never be able to face, ever…

Pictures in my Phone

Walking alone in this lonely night,
I hold on to your sweater a bit more tight,
I wonder why didn't I deserve your fight,

I won't be calling you my lover,
Our story is over,
Now I can't stay sober,

Everyday when I wake up and see,
That you are nowhere beside me,
Tell me how more fucked up can this be,

And I reach into a different timezone,,
when I remember how you left me all alone,
And now I keep staring at your pictures in my phone,

Maybe I am going insane too,
Cause I keep on talking to the ghost of you,
Tell me do you do that too,

You took a piece of me,
I let you ruin me completely,
And now I am so lonely,

Now that I am completely destroyed,
Like suddenly hit by an asteroid,
With nothing to fill this empty void,

Nothing is changed but nothing is same,

There is no fire to ignite this dead flame,
My head hanging down in shame,

They say everything is fair in war and love,
But this wasn't what they call true love,
I was just another one you wanted to get rid of,

When you left out from the back door
Didn't know it will scar me till the very core,
And I will never be like I was before,

Maybe it was supposed to end like this,
Love destroys you piece by piece,
Like free falling eternally into this abyss.

Tell me how do I get rid of those memories, tell me how do I delete it all so that they don't come haunting again when I am with someone else, when I am trying to move on, when I am trying to make peace with the fact that I will never have you again, when I will never be able to touch you again, and that I have to learn to live without you. Come in agreement with the fact that you and I, no matter how perfect we were, we weren't just meant to be. Tell me how do I stop this nostalgia where I am pulled in some kind of trance of our memories and I never want to leave, I never want to leave that illusion where everything is the way its supposed to be, where its just you and me, so tell me, how do I delete all your memory.

Curse

I never thought it will come down to this,
why did it turn into curse when it was a bliss,

I never thought you will forget me so easily,
Erasing me from your memory completely,

You even replaced my name on your phone,
While I am still writing our memories on my gravestone,

Maybe it was just another piece of cake for you,
Crushing my heart and leaving me so blue,

Painting me in shades of grey,
When I was begging you to stay,

And you had no words to say,
When you were walking away,

You walked out of my life,
Like my heart was scratched with a knife,

You left me all alone,
my heart turned into stone,

My pillow never went dry,
From the tears I used to cry,

Holding on to your blue sweater,

I would hope that it will all be better,

But I had already lost my chance,
I didn't realize it was all a trance,

You and I were just temporary,
And the world we built together was imaginary.

I walked on a very thin line, when I was walking towards you, I knew I was walking towards my doom, but I walked anyway, cause the destination seemed rather interesting than the journey and the aftermath is my own curse to bear. You see, a lifetime of pain is worth the time we spent. I will always be greedy, I will always want more, I might even walk on the paths I am not supposed to cause the end result is way better but the

History

I know I wasn't supposed to fall for you,
Doesn't mean that the love I had wasn't true,

I just wanted to be your friend,
But it wasn't in my control to discommend,

and It's not something I consider a privilege,
but trust me I wasn't thinking about my image,

Is dreaming about you considered alright,
Because you even hate my sight,

Take me back to the night we met,
And maybe we would rewrite our fate,

And though it was all written in the stars,
You were worth every scar,

You were the color to my black and white,
I am the darkness, and you were my light,

With you I just can't stop smiling,
Every word you say is mesmerizing,

And now I always feel so alone,
Cause I am devoured of my home,

Loving you with everything I had, but it was never enough,

Because I was never the one you were thinking of,

Does it hurt when you say my name,
Cause I was never your endgame,

Replaying your words in my mind again and again,
your memories have still tied me up in chain,

You and I were never meant to be,
And everything we had is distant history.

You see, you are a secret of mine, that I don't want to share with anyone else. I am selfish that way, if I could I would keep all of you to myself, but I will manage with only a small part that is supposed to be mine, kinda like my dirty little secret about which I write down in my diary, a comfort place I visit to escape this world, a secret language only we can speak and nobody has any business knowing about you cause they will never understand what we had, why all the red flags couldn't stop me, why you had the power to completely ruin me…

Kryptonite

Having a private concert at 4 am in my balcony,
Singing all the songs you introduced to me,
Crying before, during and after every song,
Nothing has ever felt so damn wrong,

The moon and the stars would witness every scene,
Till the sun would touch me where your lips had once been,
The same thing would play on repeat every night,
And your name would be my kryptonite,

The most painful ways to die seem to be so easy now,
Only if I could gather enough courage to jump from here somehow,
I don't remember the last time I slept without nightmares of you,
Cause every night my brain would find a new way to remember you,

Looking down I wondered if I could just end it all,
I wondered if I could make it look like an accidental fall,
Will i ever be able to make peace with it all being over,
Will I ever be able to accept that you and I weren't meant to be together,

Though every day I would promise myself to start a new,
But every night was a struggle just to get through,
Every moment drowning myself in agony,

Can someone please end this feeling permanently,

Maybe I wasn't as important to you as you were to me,
You were the mountains boy but I was lost at sea,
Were we just two souls never meant to meet,
And maybe in every other universe our story is incomplete,

For every star reminds me of you,
Everything I do can be traced back to you,
I might lose my way and still,
Every time I do, I find my way back to you,

And the stars don't have any answer to why is it this way,
Why is betrayal coated in every word that you ever say,
Didn't you once loved me simple and plain,
Why can't we ever be the same way again.

I sometimes wonder that if I ever hold that hand again, will I ever be able to let go, and if I have to, in how many pieces will I break this time, and in the end will I be able to put myself back together? Maybe I was the curse who wasn't meant to cross your path, cause everything around me seems to be breaking and maybe I am the reason for it all, cause you see I was never destined for good things to begin with and everything good around me gets destroys, slowly but eventually…

Numb

It still doesn't ease the pain,
knowing that we are strangers again,

Holding onto your sweater a bit more tight,
Wondering why wasn't I worth your fight,

Every night I see you in all the stars,
But you are nowhere when I stumble out of bars,

I really wish I could forget it all,
Every word said, every other phone call,

I don't want to feel this pain no more,
Can't we go back to how it was before,

my life is cold like it is hit by a comet,
I am pretty sure I will never be able to forget,

All the emotions I have is in chaos,
Even in complete silence your name echoes,

now every part of my soul feels numb,
You left me making me feel so dumb,

Every touch of yours and every memory,
Wasn't it way too easy to forget about me,

Everything felt like it is in streaks of grey,
Because you didn't had any words to say,

And everything you said to me was a lie,
turned my whole life upside down, don't even know why,

Completely destroyed now I am left in ruins,
Feels like eternal damnation for all my sins.

I still think about you in the pauses that I take, I still think of you with the smile that I fake. I still think about you in all the broken promises that were made, I still think about you in all the words left unsaid, I still think about you when I am lying alone on my bed, I still think about you with tears that I shed, I still think about you every day, I still think about you in the pauses that are made, and I guess, I can never stop...

Pause

can you hug me once tonight,
Turn every wrong into right,
Be the word to everything I write,

For I have been loving you since so long,
And I know that I was so very wrong,
But can you be the melody to my every song,

And I am not asking you to stay forever,
Just be with me in all my life's endeavor,
And I promise to be with you wherever,

Can we for a moment hit pause,
You were my favourite of all that was,
You know I loved you, just because,

And Everything seemed so easy with you,
All my feelings were completely new,
Didn't know they would leave me so blue,

Now the words wont flow,
And I don't know,
what it means anymore,

Everything reminding me of you,
All my nightmares turning true,
But am I still in love with you,

You know that I am still in love with you, and I will always keep on falling more with every talk, every word exchanged, with every eye contact and with every breath that I take. I may pretend that I even forgot your face, and that the shape of your name means nothing to me, but you have to know that I am lying and there is no possible universe in which that can happen. Cause you have left an imprint on my soul, and that will remain a part of me for all of my eternity.

Fault in our Stars

you know what never gets old,
When I am so very cold,
And you wrap your arms around me,
Slowly setting my soul free,

You know it's so sad,
That I lost everything I had,
And I lost myself too,
But it ain't worse than losing you,

why did you walk away,
loosing you was the hardest price to pay,
I still remember your smile,
I have been missing it now for a while,

I can't forget how being with you felt,
Or the way that you smelled,
And how everything seemed easier,
loosing you was my greatest fear,

Maybe those were the fault in our stars,
That we will love each other from the start,
Knight in shining armor coming to my rescue,
And then we would leave each other blue,

Memories that I can never get rid of, how is it that everyone before you seems to be a blur, I might remember their name but I definitely do not remember anything else and that is when you were not even supposed to be mine. Your smile, your eyes, your hands in mine, it takes everything in me not to come running back to you, but do you remember me the way I do, do you ever stay awake at night thinking about me, do you think of me at all, call someone else by my name when you are way too drunk to remember anything else.

Miss my smile

I was never worthy of you,
And Maybe you knew it too

Do you still take a trip down the memory lane,
Does thinking bout us still drives you insane,

You did not had to leave me all alone,
Throwing me like a tissue when you were done,

If this was love, how is it that you are okay,
While I am hurting more with each passing day,

How can I be fine,
When I cant even call you mine,

I miss all that we had,
Does thinking about us makes you sad,

I miss my smile I had when I was with you,
And everything now is in shades of grey and blue,

Do you ever think about me anytime,
When you are writing something you want to rhyme,

Can we go back to the beginning,
Because I don't like this ending,

But now that I am left here in ruins,
Everything seems pitch black ever since,

And chaos seems to be my permanent place,
Now that you don't hold me in your embrace,

I still try to find you in every person I meet
but for you I was just another person to delete,

And now that I am left in pieces,
Everything that existed ceases.

Do you ever think about me, do you ever wonder what were the things we could have done differently or have you finally started hating me for not being for with you. Do you ever get stuck in nostalgia of our memories, do you ever write about me, or have you already moved on. Tell me if it was easy, tell me if you can tell me how to do it too, cause I am still stuck on that couch with the phone in my hand, when everything turned pitch black and I haven't been able to see any light since then.

Regrets

Turning all white pages in black,
Though you are never coming back,
I still keep waiting for you there just in case,
Cause there is no going back on this one way track,

just take me back to the time we first met,
and we will write a story you won't regret,
The whole world would be jealous,
Of the story that no one will ever forget,

But it doesn't feel the same,
when you call my name,
tell me how to be friends when,
The longer we stayed the further apart we became,

The stars dont shine anymore,
And am tired of knocking on this closed door,
the world seems to be crashing down,
when I am crying alone on my bathroom floor,

You say you care but it all seems a lie,
Like every sentence has a hidden goodbye,
A message from you is all it takes,
To leave me completely crucified,

I can't get out from the loop of your thoughts,
Loving you has crossed my heart,
from the start I should have stayed away from you,
But I guess I wasn't that smart,

But does it all seem like mistake now,
Every good thing turning sad somehow,
And though we are trying to go back like before,
I guess it would be useless now.

You see, I am trying to move to every new place I can, maybe its just another desperate attempt. Maybe I will find satisfaction if I move to new places cause mentally I am still stuck where you left me. Maybe if I move enough, I will finally be able to move on, cause I am still stuck on the way you said my name, or the way you held my hand, or the way you kissed me, and by the looks of it, no matter where I reach, I will still be stuck there for a very long time...

Blue

This time when I lose you again,
I hope it won't hurt the same,
Maybe I won’t drive myself insane,
All lost and confused trying to call your name

Maybe this time you won't leave me blue,
And this time I will get a goodbye at least,
And it won't be like another deja vu,
when your name ceases to exist.

I hope this time you stick around longer,
Even if you are just a friend,
And I hope it will all seem better,
when you look back after reaching the end.

Did you ever miss me at all,
Or did you ever even think about me,
cause you left but I wasn't ready for the free fall,
Maybe it was too easy for you to set me free.

So this time if you plan on leaving,
Can you give me some warning sign,
So I won't start doubting everything I believe in,
It may take some time, but I will be fine.

Every moment spent with you was a struggle, that there will be a time when you will leave,
And I have no idea as what I should do, how am I supposed to get my mind off you,
Every second with you clicks like a time bomb, and every time I battle to somehow make it stop,
Cause I just want to spend all my time with you, wishing you would love me back the way I do,
But nothing works the way its supposed to, and nothing seems to be going right,
But out of nowhere you come to rescue, and everything seems right when I wrap my arms around you

Losing Sleep

The reason I am loosing sleep,
You weren't mine to keep,

Would I be yet another forgotten story,
In the pool of your memories,

Would I be yet another dodged bullet,
Someone so easy to forget,

Promises that meant nothing,
I just wanted to feel something,

Seconds feel like years,
Your every goodbye leaves me with never-ending tears,

That's how from my life you would tip toe,
Nobody can land a better killing blow,

Could you please put an end to this,
Could you actually kill me please,

Tell me when you said that you loved me,
Was it comparatively easier to lie to me,

Cause every word now seems a series of unending torture,
No amount of time will be able to make anything any better.

You see blaming someone else for my own stupidity would be easier isn't it, I could blame you that you let me go so easily, you were even prepared, and I know it was already something that we needed to do even if it wasn't discussed, but sometimes heart takes a little longer to accept what the brain had already known, and still asked why would I take so much time to recover when you already knew it was about to happen, yes, I should have been prepared better, it would have been easier had I not fallen in love at all, but it just wasn't in my control, and I know it still be so pathetic of me that I am still in love with you when it took you just a second to move on…

Your Name Hurts

Your name hurts,
Your memories are worse,
Tell me if it was supposed to be blessing,
How can it turn into curse..?

Your absence hurts,
Your messages are worse,
if it was supposed to be a plaything,
how did we get that serious..?

Your voice heals,
Your smile is still mysterious,
If you were supposed to be my salvation,
Why did you leave me at my worse...?

Your touch is binding,
your imprint still on my conscience,
If it was supposed to be temporary,
Why am I feeling so tenacious...?

Your name still bring back all the memories I want to get rid of, it still takes me back to a state of nostalgia where I wanna re-live every moment spent with you again, it still fills me with this uneasy feeling that I am missing something very important, that everything I have is still inadequate, everything I am is still not good enough, and that everything I do is a façade and that I am hiding under an illusion pretending to fix something permanently broken, trying to save a ship that has already sailed, trying to save everything from burning down when only ashes remained.

Remembrance

Remember when you showed me all your scars,
Remember when you told me who you really are,

Told me about your highs and your lows,
Talked about your most fatal blows,

You said you will never fall that low again,
Because you never want to relive that kind of pain,

Is it the issue with my trust,
When you say one thing but do the absolute worst,

You said you will never let it come down to this,
When you said you will rise to stars but fell into abyss,

You assume, no one is here for you,
But one word from you and people be dying for you,

I wish that it could have been accounted for something,
When you casually say that your life means nothing,

That's a pain I could never endure,
Tears are falling, but why I am not so sure,

Did you ever consider me someone,
When you left me like I was no one,

And it might never make any sense to you,
That some people worry about what you do,

So can you do me a favor and take care of yourself,
I am pretty sure it will be considered of great help,

Because to some, you are more important than you think,
Life is very short and would end before you can blink,

But if you wish to feel any pain,
Try falling in love again,

And I hope next time you do not gather enough courage,
Before you do yourself some permanent damage.

You loved me and I loved you, but it wasn't enough,
Yeah, my thoughts were a little crazy when I was drunk,
Remember when you couldn't look me in the eyes,
Remember when we could never say our goodbyes,
Remember how you walked away like we were never meant to be,
I guess it was easier to treat me like a complete nobody...

Strangers Again

Your words don't have the feel,
And your eyes feel empty,
Maybe you still care about me,
but that's just basic humanity,

Your touch feels strange,
Like your atoms have forgotten mine,
And when you wrap me in your arms,
Your eyes don't shine,

Your hug doesn't feel the same,
And your gaze doesn't feel electrifying,
Remember when I pretended to not care about you,
I was clearly lying,

And I am just staring at you,
Trying to find the person I knew,
And the person in front of me, looks like you,
But why does he not feel like you,

The sweetest smile still exists,
But now it feels covered in guilt,
Like I am trying to ask you something,
You can never give,

And your hands don't fit in mine anymore,
But the crave to hold them is still there,
You look at me like I am a stranger,
And the love you once held isn't there,

When I still stare in your eyes,
But the love it once had is missing,
I wished you would look at me like old times,
But that's just wishful thinking.

I never thought forgetting someone would be this difficult, how is it that even if I rip myself apart, a part of you always stays with me, Even If I tear myself in a billion pieces, every piece would still have traces of you, I can turn my world upside down, and still you would be my stable ground, In this ever changing world, how are you my only constant, In this world where I hate almost everything, how did I fall in love with you...

Acknowledgements:

I would like to start with the two strongest pillars of my life, Gauri and Abhi, no matter what I was going through, you guys always stood by me through all your words and time. Thank you for standing by my side, no matter how shitty the process, life and the poems got, and also thank you for giving me permission to use your pics at some places, you guys have no idea how much this means to me.

A big thanks to Koushik and Prashant for the words of encouragement whenever I shared any piece and showing my mistakes wherever they were. I would be eternally thankful.

I would also like to thank Akshata, Yogeshwari and Dipika, to encourage me to keep writing and tolerating all of my moodiness and drama and encouraging me to write.

Next I would be thanking my permanents, Mohit, Rishabh, Yateen and Upasana, cause no matter where we are and what we will be doing, we will always be there for each other, hopefully.

And lastly the foundations of my existence, my Parents, without them, none of this would have been possible.

Special Thanks to the publisher.